Carlene Thie

HOMECOMING
Destination Disneyland

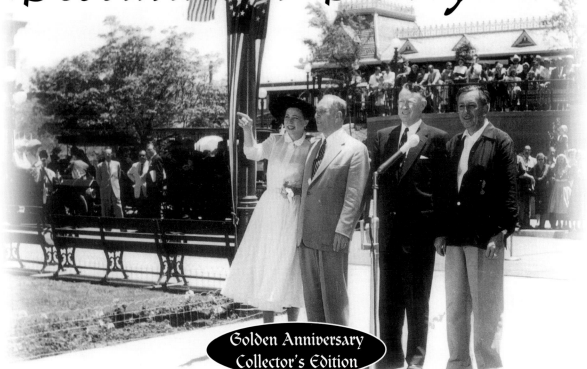

*Golden Anniversary
Collector's Edition*

Foreword by Keith Murdoch

Contributions from:

Wally Boag, Tim Conway, Tommy Cole, Ron Dias, Lisa Davis, Ron Dominguez, Richard Fleischer, Beverly Gracey, Willie Ito, Dean Jones, Ollie Johnston, Don Knotts, Art Linkletter, Jack Lindquist, Keith Murdoch, Lucille Martin, Brian McKim, Matt McKim, Sam McKim, Floyd Norman, Fess Parker, David Pacheco, Teller and Ilene Woods

Written by
Carlene Thie

Photographs by
Mell Kilpatrick

HOMECOMING
Destination Disneyland

Golden Anniversary
Collector's Edition
Second Printing

A tribute to Walt Disney's dreams and imagination.

Ape Pen Publishing LLC
Copyright © 2005

Ape Pen Publishing
P.O. Box 691
Riverside, CA 95202

Library of Congress Cataloging-in-Publication Data

Thie, Carlene.
        Homecoming Destination Disneyland / Carlene Thie,
        edited by Carolyn Burns Bass, Collector's Edition, second printing.

Library of Congress Control Number: 2004098128

ISBN: 0971793247

Cover photo tinting by Richard and Christine Sparks. www.sparksarts.com
Vellum overlay drawings by Brian McKim.

Table of Contents

Acknowledgments:
Artwork by Walt Disney, Ron Dias, Ollie Johnston,
Willie Ito, Floyd Norman, David Pacheco, Brian McKim,
and Sam McKim

Edited by: Carolyn Burns Bass

Special thanks to my loving and supportive husband John Thie
and my good friends Patrick Jenkins and Carolyn Burns Bass.

A Tribute to My Grandfather, Mell Kilpatrick

My grandfather, Mell Kilpatrick, had a sense of history and a passion for photography. Both of these pursuits led him to take what started as a hobby and turn it into a profession that led him to become the chief photographer for the Santa Ana Register. Using his Speed Graphic camera, Mell shot the streets of Orange County, documenting everything from car accidents to crime scenes. He recorded a nascent Orange County where Interstate 5 was a state highway snaking through (then called Highway 101), where vast tracts of orange groves were flattened one day and built up the next. It was from these orange groves that Mell recorded one of Orange County's defining monuments... Disneyland.

Mell worked relentlessly to capture in film Walt's Disney dream. Mell climbed atop scaffolding, he crawled into tunnels, he even hung out of a light plane 5,000 feet above Disneyland to snap the perfect shot. Like any momentous project, Disneyland under construction was sometimes chaotic and many of the features, such as a darkroom, were low priority. When he found out that Walt needed a local place to develop staff photos, Mell opened his darkroom to official Disney photographers for developing the park's first images. Walt often called Mell to come photograph special days during construction, as well as granting Mell unlimited access to Disneyland. Along with dozens of the nation's photographers, Mell was invited to photograph Disneyland's Golden opening day. History buff that he was, Mell saved every piece of memorabilia from that day, including the official Disneyland Press Kit.

Mell was only sixty years old in 1962 when a heart attack claimed his life. His prized darkroom was locked and left undisturbed for thirty years. Through the years, I began to appreciate all of the old things and memorabilia my grandmother had saved. She knew I appreciated the stories attached to the memorabilia, not just the keepsakes themselves. Reminiscing about my grandfather and his passion for photography, she often took me into the neglected darkroom. There in the dim, musty room, my grandmother and I sorted through the dusty stacks of photographs, many of them brown and brittle with age. I marveled at the vintage black and white images of Orange County and compared them to the four-color world outside the darkroom. And I loved to hear her stories about my grandfather, their life, and his love of photography.

Several years after my grandmother died and left me all of my grandfather's photos, I decided to see if other people had similar interests in vintage photography and especially my grandfather's treasure: his collection of historic Disneyland photos. Some quick web surfing satisfied my curiosity. Not only did I find scores of people interested in vintage photography, but also a very dedicated group of people who appreciate the work of Walt Disney and his vision for Disneyland. One of the people I met online suggested that I take a sample of the Disney photos to a Disney show and mark people's response to them. Blessed by the response of how many people shared my interest, I resolved to make them available for people to purchase.

The enthusiasm and demand for the photos continued, many people suggesting that I publish the photos in a book to make the collection accessible. Until I began this project, I had never considered writing a book and didn't know how to go about publishing. But as the granddaughter of a self-starting entrepreneur, I began my own publishing company. Named after my dog, April, Ape Pen Publishing was born. In March 2001 my first book was published: *A Photographer's Life with Disneyland Under Construction.* With the warm acceptance of the book and the encouragement of so many people, I decided to continue sharing my grandfather's photos. Within the next two years I published three more books of vintage Disneyland photos. By May of 2004 all four books were a permanent part of Disneyland's landscape of merchandise. In 2005 *Homecoming Destination Disneyland* became part of Disneyland's 50th anniversary merchandise.

During the wonderful journey of researching and publishing these books, I found so much reward in my grandmother's stories. Not only did my grandfather shoot photos during Disneyland's infancy, but my father worked in constructing major parts of Disneyland, and my grandmother worked at Disneyland for 18 years. I discovered that my grandfather had a special relationship with Walt Disney. Walt admired Mell's work and Mell respected Walt and his dreams. Walt Disney's dream opened on July 17, 1955 and Mell Killpatrick was there to capture the day.

Thanks to Mell, these historic images will last for generations. My hope is that these books capture the wonder of Disneyland, the dreams of the beloved Walt Disney, and the creativity of my grandfather Mell Kilpatrick.

Carlene Thie

Finding Disneyland
Foreword by Keith Murdoch
Former City Manager of Anaheim, California

Photo courtesy of Keith Murdoch

As Anaheim City Manager, my first involvement with the Disney search occurred following the Anaheim Halloween Parade in October 1953. Earnie Moeller, manager of the Anaheim Chamber of Commerce, customarily included representatives of industries which might be induced to locate in the city. One judge was Nat Wyckoff who represented Walt Disney. I was usually invited to meet and co-host the judges.

After the judging was complete, Earnie called me aside to meet with Nat. The three of us sat in a car in the alley next to the chamber office building where Nat told me that they were considering an Anaheim area location for a Disneyland amusement park, but they had run into some trouble with the site recommended by their consultant. Earnie and I agreed we would look for suitable alternatives and get back to Nat ASAP.

We outlined two likely sites which met Disney's criteria of about 160 acres near to, and accessible from, a freeway. One was along the west side of Euclid north from Ball Road; La Palma, Magnolia, Crescent and Gilbert circled the other. Both sites were mainly orange groves with a few buildings. Walt Disney was interested and arranged to tour the site the following Saturday morning. Walt and several of his staff picked the two of us up with their station wagon and off we went to Euclid.

Shortly before reaching the first site, we passed a rather unkempt cemetery. Walt said, "What's that?" in a very disapproving manner. We explained, but Walt was not satisfied and replied, "I wouldn't bring my guests past this for love nor money. Do you have another site?" So we took the group to the other site. They liked that one.

Earnie and I returned home, and the Disney group went to Knott's Berry Farm for lunch and a discussion of the site and their plans to start obtaining the properties on Monday. Unfortunately, at an adjacent table, there was a realtor from Garden Grove. He was all ears listing to the description. The next day, Sunday, he obtained listings on a few of the key parcels. When Disney found out about that action, he was infuriated and decided not to proceed.

Back to the drawing board, and our search began. The next site was a little smaller on the north side of La Palma between Magnolia and Gilbert. I don't know why that one failed to materialize, but a larger site east of Brookhurst running north from La Palma to Huston St (now replaced by the 91 freeway) came up. This was available as a package from cooperative owners.

However, one of Disney's stockholders filed suit, maintaining that the corporation did not have the authority to build and operate an amusement park. By the time Disney was able to correct that legal barrier, the properties had been sold to a housing developer and were no longer available for the park.

Now we were out of sites! But this was too big of a project to give up. One Sunday afternoon, I sat alone in my office staring at a large map on the wall, which showed all of the land parcels and their ownership for Northern Orange County. Besides proximity to a freeway, one of the requirements was that obstructions such as power lines couldn't be in direct line from the park to Mt. Wilson. Disney wanted to be clear to televise programs from the park. The technology at that time required a clear shot. I looked again at the original preferred site and by staying north of the power lines, a sufficient parcel was available. But Cerritos Ave, a street that went from Harbor Boulevard all the way to the Pacific Ocean, was in the middle of it. I said to myself "wait a minute. We have closed streets in the city for beneficial purposes, why not this one?" Since the properties were still in unincorporated territory, the procedure might be different. So I turned to the municipal law books against the wall and read the procedures required. If the residents and the landowners along the street were willing to sell, then they should also approve abandonment of a no longer necessary street. Bingo! I called Earnie with the suggestions that I had found a site. He hurried to the office and I showed him the location. I pointed out that the street would have to be abandoned. "Can you do that?" He gasped. I assured him that it could be done with willing property owners.

The next morning, Earnie called Disney and set up a meeting with Walt and his key people in Burbank. When we presented the proposal, which was so close to the one pin pointed by the consultant firm, Stanford Research Institute, the group was excited, but the street abandonment was critical. Walt's query was the same as Earnie's, "Can you do that?" After a brief explanation and assurance was given, Walt said, "If you can close that street, we've got a deal," and a handshake deal was made.

Several times during the construction period I had the opportunity to meet with Walt and usually Roy Disney, sometimes at Walt's office at the Burbank Studio and sometimes at the park construction. If Walt would get carried away in enthusiastically discussing a subject and appear too pompous to Roy, Roy would gently remind Walt of their first arrival in California with only twenty dollars between them. Walt's familiar sheepish grin would take over, and the conversation would continue. Those experiences impressed upon me the sincere nature of the Disneys.

Walt would come out to the park while it was under construction if he was in the area. One of his hobbies was railroad steam engines. When things were to be built, obviously he had to have a railroad. While they were building the railroad around the berm he'd walk that track and shake his head and say something's wrong. Finally, Walt figured out what apparently was wrong. In between the tracks were a bunch of rocks around the railroad, it was called ballast. And the ballast is crushed rock. And he looked at that crushed rock and said, "That's not to scale. It gives a wrong appearance." So we had the ballast, that had already been installed, removed, crushed to scale, and replaced. Walt would watch every detail. His perception was wonderful.

It was exciting to watch the construction and everything. I marvel at the ingenuity of the Disney imagineers with Marty Sklar at the helm to implement and expand Walt's dreams. The castle, for instance, is built in perspective to appear taller than it is. You may notice that the masonry blocks at the base are larger than the next row. Then there is Walt's favorite number 13. So when it came to assigning of address numbers to Disneyland, the inspector tried to figure out where 1313 might be and it happened to be right about in the middle of the freeway. Walt said you'll assign it to Disneyland.

On opening day Walt had invited a lot of people, primarily press, but a lot of other people. Their invitations stated, "For you and your party." Some of those parties got to be 30 or 40 people. So that meant there was a greater crowd than what they had anticipated and traffic was actually backed up on the freeway. Walt later called it Black Sunday.

There were all kinds of moments to consider and all kinds of possible failures and so on. I love having the memory of Walt, and that's pretty full.

Aerial view of Adventureland and Main Street

Main Street and surrounding lands starting to take shape

Building A Dream

A press release reproduced from the original Disneyland Opening Day press kit, 1955

Public Relations Dept.
Disneyland, Inc.
1313 Harbor Blvd.
Anaheim, Calif.

Exactly one year and one day after breaking ground on a 160 acre orange grove in Anaheim, Calif., Disneyland, Walt Disney's multimillion dollar magic kingdom, opens to the public.

With this July 18 inaugural, Walt Disney realizes a life-time dream in offering Disneyland to the young of all ages to experience active delights of the moment, to savor the challenge and promise of the future, and to older generations to relive fond memories of the past.

For over 20 years--almost from the time Mickey Mouse's voice was heard across the world--Walt Disney envisioned a "magic kingdom" that would create a whole lavish new kind of entertainment designed for family participation, based upon his own wonderful characters.

His original plans was to build the park on the studio lot in Burbank. However, as his cartoon family and other activities grew, so did the dream and it soon became apparent that something far larger than the Burbank lot was necessary.

Since location of this unique park was of prime importance, Disney retained the Stanford Research Institute in June, 1953, to make an extensive site and location study. The Stanford project was under the direction of C. V. Wood, Jr. After the survey was completed Wood was assigned by Walt to act as Vice President and General Manager of Disneyland, Inc., to continue with actual construction and organization.

Selection of the site was made from among many after a year's study in location analysis and a complete search of land records. Among other qualifications, utility conditions, accessibility, topography and environmental characteristics were considered. Even annual rainfall figures

<u>BUILDING A DREAM</u>

Public Relations Dept.
Disneyland, Inc.
1313 Harbor Blvd.
Anaheim, Calif.

helped in making the final decision.

During this period Stanford Research conducted a complete economic feasibility study of the entire Disneyland operation. This included a thorough survey of attendance patterns for amusement areas and the projection of an annual rate of operation for Disneyland.

In designing and building Disneyland, nothing was left to chance.

When Walt began to put his ideas into sketches the amount of research and technical data required seemed almost impossible.

By the time the property had been purchased and ground broken, scouting teams were traveling over the United States and Canada to secure authentic equipment for Walt Disney's grand project.

It took three cities to supply the 100-year-old gas lamps that line Main Street. They are set aglow each evening at dusk by a lamplighter, a relic of the turn of the century.

Some of the cresting and railing that is seen in Frontierland and Main Street came from old plantations in Nashville and Memphis, Tenn., and some came from San Francisco, Oakland and Sacramento, dating back to the '49 days.

Part of the marine equipment--used only for exhibit purposes at Frontierland Park--consists of an old anchor which was found in an antique shop in New Orleans, and thought to be about 200 years old. It is believed to have been a part of a pirate ship--possibly Jean LaFitte's.

Because all construction was on 5/8 scale, mills across the nation were contacted for special narrow-striped awning and umbrella materials.

Building A Dream

1955 Public Opening Day

Opening: Monday, July 18, 1955 at 10 a.m.

Location: 1313 Harbor Boulevard, in Anaheim, California

Hours: 10 a.m. to 10 p.m. seven days a week during the summer. Open 6 days a week in the fall, closed on Mondays.

Founder: Walt Disney

Area Size: Total area: 160 acres. Park: 60 acres.

Parking: Parking lot size: 100 acres. Car capacity: 12,175.

Admission: $1.00, including tax, for adults and 50 cents, including tax, for children 12 and under.

Food: 20 restaurants in all the four different lands.

Walking: To visit every land, distance of 1.4 miles.

Personnel: Over 1,000 employees.

Capacity: Designed to handle 60,000 visitors daily.

Landscaping: Plants from all over the world. Approximately 12,000 orange trees removed.

Gov. & Mrs. Knight, Walt and Rev. Glenn Puder on Opening Day

The raising of the American flag during Opening Day ceremony

Walt rides with California Governor Knight in Opening Day parade

Independently driven Autopia cars in Opening Day parade

Public Relations Dept.
Disneyland, Inc.
1313 Harbor Blvd.
Anaheim, Calif.

A creative genius who has the capacity to make his dreams come true, Walt Disney has made his biggest one a reality. He envisioned a play-ground for people of all ages that would become a source of joy and in-spiration to everyone who came to see it.

The result is Disneyland, a $17,000,000 park in Anaheim, Calif., dedicated to happiness and knowledge--a land where fantasy and imagination are companions with history, and a concrete visualization of the future is not out of place. This wide range of imaginative reality is in keeping with the Disney scope of activities and is typical of the man himself.

When he came to Hollywood in 1923, Walt Disney's assets consisted of $40.00 in cash and a boundless imagination. He and his brother Roy, a partner in all Walt's ventures, including Disneyland, managed to borrow enough money from an uncle to set up a cartoon studio back of a real estate office. Later--much later--he was dealing in millions to set up Disney-land, his grandest venture in public entertainment.

The creator of Mickey Mouse and founder of Disneyland was born in Chicago, Dec. 5, 1901. His father was Elias Disney, Irish-Canadian; and his mother, Flora Call Disney, was of German-American descent. He has three brothers and a sister. He went to public school in Chicago and Kansas City and attended art school in Chicago. He is married to the former Lillian Bounds of Idaho. They have two daughters--Diane and Sharon. Diane is married to former S. C. football star, Ron Miller. The Millers recently made Walt a proud grandfather upon the birth of their son, Christopher Disney Miller. Sharon, the youngest daughter, is a student at the University of Arizona.

-more-

Walt Disney Biography

A press release reproduced from the original Disneyland Opening Day press kit, 1955

Walt Disney's Biography

WALT DISNEY BIOGRAPHY

Public Relations Dept.
Disneyland, Inc.
1313 Harbor Blvd.
Anaheim, Calif.

Both Walt and his wife enjoy moving pictures and in his Holmby Hills home he has complete projection equipment and runs pictures three and four nights a week. Walt is also one of the nation's most ardent railroading fans. His interest in this diversion ranges from miniature equipment to scale model operation on track laid around his Holmby Hills estate. Railroading elements often are incorporated in his pictures, and two 5/8 scale locomotives, pulling six cars each, are in daily operation at Disneyland as the Santa Fe and Disneyland Railroad.

In business, Walter Elias Disney has been a life-long partner with his elder brother, Roy, president of Walt Disney Productions.

When the Disney brothers first set up shop, Walt's proficiency as an artist and a self-taught animator was the basis of the undertaking-- the founding of an institution which today is housed in a multi-million dollar studio in Burbank, Calif.

Although not his first cartoon character, it was Mickey Mouse, destined to become a continuously famous movie star, who marked Walt Disney has a genius of entertainment. "Silly Symphonies," a series of brilliant short musi-comedies, came next. In 1937 "Snow White" set a new pattern in the feature-length field.

When World War II broke out, scores of highly trained Disney technicians streamed into every branch of the armed service, and the studio turned unreservedly to the service of Uncle Sam. Ninety-four per cent of the Disney facilities became engaged in special government work, while the remainder was devoted to the production of cartoon subjects, deemed highly essential to civilian and military morale.

3

WALT DISNEY BIOGRAPHY

Public Relations Dept.
Disneyland, Inc.
1313 Harbor Blvd.
Anaheim, Calif.

The first post-war feature was a musical, "Make Mine Music," which highlighted a new Disney idea -- the voices and talents of screen luminaries, used in combination with the cartoon medium.

Then came "Song of the South," "Fun and Fancy Free," "So Dear To My Heart," "Ichabod and Mr. Toad," "Treasure Island," "Cinderella," "Alice In Wonderland," "The Story of Robin Hood," "Peter Pan," "The Sword and the Rose," "Rob Roy, the Highland Rogue," and "20,000 Leagues Under the Sea."

"Lady and the Tramp," the first feature-length animated cartoon in CinemaScope, went into release in 1955 after three years of intensive production. Two of his latest live-action features are "Davy Crockett, King of the Wild Frontier," recently released, and "The Littlest Outlaw," to be released this year.

"Sleeping Beauty" is currently in production and is scheduled for release sometime in 1957.

One of Walt Disney's sensational new contributions to popular screen entertainment is the True-Life Adventure series of factual films in nature's own colors and authentic settings. Seven, topped by "The Living Desert" and "The Vanishing Prairie" have won annual Academy Awards in their category. This year "The African Lion" will be candidate for another Oscar.

In addition to his motion picture activities, Disney has entered the television field on a grand scale. In October, 1954, "Disneyland," a weekly hour-long show was launched over ABC-TV. Within a few weeks it jumped to one of the top ten shows in the nation. Divided into four

Walt Disney's Biography

WALT DISNEY BIOGRAPHY

Public Relations Dept.
Disneyland, Inc.
1313 Harbor Blvd.
Anaheim, Calif.

alternating segments--"Fantasyland," "Adventureland," "Frontierland," and "Tomorrowland,"--shows emanate from one of these four realms on succeeding weeks.

With the success of the weekly show, ABC contracted with Walt for a new hour-long daily television show, Monday through Friday, designed for the youngsters. The fall of 1955 launches "The Mickey Mouse Club," along with a continuation of the weekly show, "Disneyland," which received its title and format from the 60 acre "magic kingdom" in Anaheim, Calif.

Plans for this wonderland first began to go on paper as far back as 1932 when Walt's magnificent dream began to take form. In cleaning out files at the Burbank studio recently, original Disneyland sketches, bearing the 1932 date, were found.

The opening of this magic kingdom on July 18, 1955, marked the pinnacle of a life-long dream for its creator, Walt Disney, who described it as "a fabulous playground--something of a fair, a city from the Arabian Nights, a metropolis of the future, a show place of magic and living facts, but above all, a place for people to find happiness and knowledge.

#

Walt Disney's Biography

Main Street alive with activity

Main Street Station beginning to take shape

Main Street painting crew including Mell Kilpatrick's son-in-law Blaine Sissel (1st on right)

Progress on Main Street

Looking down Main Street through clock tower

Fess Parker greets journalists previewing Disneyland construction

Fess Parker and Buddy Ebsen

Disneyland starting to take shape

Mickey Mouse peeks from the now famous main gate planter

Ron Dominguez

One of the original landowners from whom
Walt Disney purchased land for the park
Began working at Disneyland in 1955
Former Executive Vice President of Disneyland

Paul Sr., Paul Jr., Laura and Ron in 1950
Photo courtesy of Ron Dominguez

Being a native Californian, a native Anaheimer, I've seen a lot of changes over the years. From the sleepy community of Anaheim arose Disneyland.

I grew up in the orange groves that surrounded downtown Anaheim. That was when Orange County was probably the orange capital of the world, or at least of the United States back in the '40s and '50s. It was a fun community to grow up in.

Both of my parents were born and raised in the Anaheim area. My Mom was born in 1898 on the property where Disneyland is located. Her grandfather came to Anaheim in probably the early 1890s and met my grandmother.

Anaheim was the lucky city chosen to bring Disneyland to reality, thanks to the help of a lot of people in the community. The Anaheim City Manager Keith Murdock played a big role in making sure that Anaheim was the chosen spot.

The original acquisition was supposed to be from Ball Road south to Cerritos Avenue. When it came to this parcel my Mom had a tough time trying to reach agreement on selling. In the first package we were going to carve out a 200 x 200 piece of property and she was going to stay in this piece of property that she grew up on. There was a lot of sentiment for her to leave the property that she and her mother had grown up on. The first concept of a 200 x 200 lot for her to live on ended up being a problem with getting a clear title on property, so therefore it wouldn't work. She was a pretty smart lady in her way of realizing things had to move ahead. Times change, things had to advance, communities have to grow. So she conceded along with all of the other 17 families and the property was sold in probably early '53.

In those early days, particularly on weekends, we'd see this big, black limousine or Cadillac or Lincoln (whatever type car it was), driving around real slow and they'd stop at each home and look at the property and look at the surroundings. Not knowing who that person was in the car, we figured it must be whoever was buying the property. We really didn't know until maybe a year out exactly who it was: Walt Disney, and probably Roy Disney along with him. One of the real estate people, Ed Wagner, was a good friend of my folks and he gave us an insight into who was buying the property and what he was trying to do. It's too bad that Walt didn't stop, get out and say, "Hey, I'm the guy."

After the deal was put to bed and all of the information became public, the Disney Company invited all of the local community business people and city fathers and the landowners up to the Walt Disney Studios to view what was planned for this thing in Anaheim. Everybody was quite comfortable with Walt's approach to Disneyland and his ideas of how to operate it and maintain it. Everybody felt assured that they weren't getting a circus moving into town that would be gone in a year.

Construction started in July of 1954. They had marked some trees and came through and said they were going to save this tree and store these, and so on. In the general vicinity of the grist mill on Tom Sawyer Island and somewhere between the entrance to Pirates of the Caribbean and the Rivers of America is where our home and our ten acres of oranges groves was located. The palm tree that sat in front of our house was moved and relocated to the Jungle Cruise. It was a wedding gift to my grandparents back in the 1890s. And it's still there.

12171 Cerritos Ave.
Photo courtesy of Ron Dominguez

Opening day was one of those hectic days. I was a ticket taker at the main gate. That was my first job. They planned for people to come to Disneyland in waves for the first two or three days. A group was invited for 9:00 in the morning. The other groups would be at staggered arrival times. Well, that didn't really work, because nobody wanted to miss a thing. Those that were due to come in the afternoon were there early in the morning waiting their turn. They didn't want to miss all the celebrities like Frank Sinatra, Sammy Davis, Jr., Art Linkletter, and Ronald Reagan—some of the emcees coming out to the sleepy little town of Anaheim for this grand opening of Disneyland.

Disneyland survived and made it through the first day without too many hitches. There was criticism for no drinking fountains. There had been a plumbing strike during the construction days and so they didn't have a chance to get all the drinking fountains in and so people thought that Walt was trying to sell Coke and soft drinks, rather than having some water for people, but that wasn't the story. The asphalt was a little soft at times, and ladies in high heels would stick in the soft asphalt because it had just been laid practically that morning or late the night before, so it hadn't had a chance to set up for the opening day of July 17th, 1955. Other than a few hitches like that, and a gas leak up at the castle that had to evacuate everybody for a short period of time, everyone survived and Disneyland made it through that first day.

I took a summer job at Disneyland, and it lasted for almost 40 years. There was a time I thought I was going to leave in 1955 after my first summer. My boss talked me into sticking around. I'm really proud that I stayed. It changed my life. I originally wanted to be a pharmacist, that's where I thought I was headed in my life. It was a great career and it was unbelievable.

On several occasions in my early days, I met Walt when he would walk through the park on Sunday afternoons. He'd stop by to see how things were going. I was in a supervisory position on Main Street in 1956 when we had just brought out the Omni Bus. I was in the back area of the Omni Bus with a little mechanical problem and Walt walked up and said, "Well, Ron, what do you think of the Omni Bus?"

Being honest, I said, "Well, I think it looks a little big on Main Street. It looks a little out of scale."

Walt replied, "I think it looks damn good."

He converted me real quick I guess, because I said, "Oh, I guess you're right, sir." That was my first encounter with him just asking my opinion.

Walt would spend a lot of time at the park on weekends coming back from Palm Springs. He would pop in and wander around. He would sometimes walk in the back areas and then out on stage, until somebody would recognize him and then he'd slip backstage. But you could tell when he was being creative and trying to dream and think up new ideas about what would be next for Disneyland. Then other times he was just wanting to talk and get your opinion on things. He was easy to talk to and a very easy person to communicate with.

The detail that Walt put into Disneyland is just unbelievable. I remember one time that he was taking a tour with the designers and there was a little building and it had some stained glass in it. Somebody said, "Well, Walt, we don't have to put stained glass in there. It could be just colored glass, because nobody could tell the difference."

He says, "I would. I would know the difference."

That's what makes Disneyland special, that he was so conscious of detail. Walt told that story at our tenth anniversary party awards banquet for all of us who had been there ten years, Walt and Roy both came down for the event.

Walt was a remarkable person, and for my parents, especially for my mother who was so sentimental about the property. She was very proud of what Disneyland became.

Ron Dominguez

A Visit
to Disneyland

*A press release reproduced
from the original Disneyland
Opening Day press kit, 1955.*

A VISIT TO DISNEYLAND

Public Relations Dept.
Disneyland, Inc.
1313 Harbor Blvd.
Anaheim, Calif.

Turn back the clock 50 years when you enter the Main Street of Disneyland in Anaheim, Calif., and look down the "heartline of America" as it appeared at the turn of the century.

As you enter this $17,000,000 wonderland the cares of today are left behind and the Walt Disney magic is apparent everywhere.

Main Street itself is a replica of a typical street of a small town in the United States about 1900. Its leisurely pace is set by the horse-drawn street cars stopping to pick up and discharge passengers in the friendly, unhurried fashion of yesterday.

Coming through the railroad station, from which all Disneyland traffic stems, the Town Square gets first attention. To the right is the Opera House and across the Square is City Hall. The fire station houses a horse-drawn hose and chemical wagon.

Looking up Main Street, the Emporium is busy with shoppers who are actually making purchases. Customers transact business at the bank, photo shop, meat market and drug store. Others visit the Penny Arcade. Some stop in for refreshment at the old-fashioned Ice Cream Parlor where marble top tables and wire back chairs preserve the atmosphere of the period. A lamplighter sets old-time gas lights aglow at twilight.

At the end of Main Street is the Plaza, Disneyland's hub, from which any of the lands may be entered. Here also, are two large restaurants. One is the Plaza Pavilion where guests may serve themselves and take their food, in paper containers, to a table on the lawn in front. The other is a Delmonico-style restaurant, the Red Wagon Inn, of the gay nineties period. Interior paneling, stairway, and crystal chandeliers for this

A VISIT TO DISNEYLAND

Public Relations Dept.
Disneyland, Inc.
1313 Harbor Blvd.
Anaheim, Calif.

restaurant were taken from an old mansion which was bought and dismantled for this purpose.

Looking to the right at the Plaza is Tomorrowland where a swift time transition takes place and the calendar rolls ahead to 1986. At the entrance to this land of the future a huge clock gives the time any place on earth. Exciting exhibits of scientific conquest and achievements to come are presented. Transportation and communication as they may be many years hence, entertainment of future generations--even food service and techniques are shown as they probably will be in half a century.

In Tomorrowland the three billion year story of the universe is shown--from the time earth was a flaming globe whirling endlessly through space. The "Story of Oil" from yesterday into tomorrow is an exciting industrial exhibit with a 40 foot diorama of the Los Angeles area for the setting.

One of the most exciting, as well as scientifically accurate, rides in Tomorrowland is the TWA "Rocket to the Moon." This ride may be taken on the "Luna" or the "Diana." Either ship accommodates 104 passengers for a seven minute simulated excursion into space. On this journey passengers experience the powerful thrust of a jet take-off, the whine of rushing air, and then the utter quiet of hurtling, faster than sound, toward the moon. Traveling at 38 miles per second, you reverse direction and begin to brake for reduced speed.

Another simulated aerial adventure is the Disneyland Space Station X-1. Its passengers view America from a space station traveling in an orbit 500 miles above the earth's surface.

A Visit to Disneyland

continued on page 124

Aerial view from parking lot

Group photo in front of Main Street Train Station

View of Town Square from the Opera House

Jack Lindquist and Walt Disney cruising in Christmas parade

Photo courtesy of Jack Lindquist

Jack Lindquist
Advertising Manager, 1955
President of Disneyland, 1989-1994

At an awards banquet in 1989 it was announced that effective tonight, Jack Lindquist is the president of Disneyland. It was a complete surprise to me because we never had a president at Disneyland. I thought it was the best job in the world and there's just no better job.

I was at Disneyland on the opening day, totally thrilled to be able to be there with my family. It was a really hot day in July and the freeway wasn't completed. When we got there the parking lot was packed, but we finally got parked. We went up to the gate and the tickets I had were for 1:00 so you had to wait outside until 1:00. There had to be to 20,000 people in the park that day.

We referred to opening day at Disneyland as Black Sunday because it was a miserable guest experience. It was rough on the people who were working. On Main Street the asphalt hadn't really set and being a hot day, women with high heels would totally sink into the asphalt. Another big problem was there had been a plumbing strike and Walt had a decision on either to have toilets or drinking fountains. And he very wisely voted for toilets. There was one drinking fountain in all of Disneyland and that was a real trial.

The media was pretty scathing in their reports of opening day—what a mess it was, how crowded, not enough crew, and not enough drinking fountains. Eddie Mack, who was the manager of publicity at that time, set out to get every person, every reporter who was there on opening day back again to show them how we improved; and that we weren't nearly as bad as they said we were opening day. And it worked, he got them back and we turned the media around.

You know it wasn't until about 1957 that Walt and Roy and even the people that worked there were really sure it was going to work. Everyone was very dedicated to Disneyland, but there were days those first couple of years in December, February, when if we had 3,000 people we were lucky.

On Thursdays we would get paid and while there was no hard and fast rule, Walt basically asked if we could do it without hurting ourselves not to cash our checks until Monday because it was important to get the receipts from the box office over the weekend deposited into the bank to cover the payroll.

I don't think anybody really thought Disneyland would become what it is now. The thing that impressed me the most about Walt was that he had a whole lot of ideas, and he went ahead and did them. He used all the money he had and then borrowed or came up with ways to get other people to invest. And he never asked for special favors from the city or the state or the federal government. He bet everything he had on things like Snow White, on Disneyland. He believed in it, and did it. Spending his career working on it and the public loved it. I think that's amazing.

I remember Walt didn't believe my name was Jack. He always called me Bob. I would wear a little nametag that would say Jack on it, and Walt would say, hey Bob, let's do this. I was in a meeting one time with Walt and Card Walker, who at that time was vice-president of marketing for Walt Disney Productions. And we're talking about something and Walt says, "Oh, Bob, what do you think?"

Before I could answer, Card said, "Walt, that's Jack."

And Walt looked at me, and that eyebrow was way up in the air, and he turned back to Card and he said, "Looks like a Bob to me."

My feeling was, he could call me anything.

Walt was a funny guy and remarkable. He did things nobody else thought he could do. Walt was a delightful guy to work for, because he listened to you, he might not buy it, but he'd listen to you. There was no doubt who ran Disneyland: Walt Disney.

Jack Lindquist

Disneyland Emporium from Town Square

Mouseketeers enjoying Christmas parade
(Left to Right: Darlene, Lonnie, Bobby and Annette)

Tommy Cole
Original Mouseketter

I can still remember the magic. I started performing as a Mouseketeer in 1955. I performed in different parts of Disneyland. There was the Space Stage for three years and then over to Videopolis by It's a Small World.

Being a Mouseketeer was a very special part of my life. I can still remember the areas and even the smell of the popcorn. I can remember the things that went on in the dressing rooms, putting on our makeup for a show, getting dressed and stretching out so we didn't kill ourselves. There is a lot of history there and a lot of memories. I'm very fortunate for everything.

I spent four years as a Mouseketeer and to this date Disneyland still has the magic when I walk in. The first time I saw Disneyland was on opening day. They took us out there by bus to dance in rhythm down Main Street. The original Mickey Mouse Club cast was Jimmy Dodd, Sharon Baird, Bobby Burgess, Lonnie Burr, Tommy Cole, Annette Funicello, Darlene Gillespie, Cubby O'Brien, Karen Pendleton, Doreen Tracy, and Roy Williams.

I feel like I spent half my lifetime at Disneyland. For every weekend during the holidays we were shooting and when we weren't shooting Mickey Mouse Club, we were performing or signing autographs. It was a very exciting time to be on a hit show as a kid, and to be recognized.

Our first schoolroom where they would tutor us was above the fire station in Disneyland. It was close to Walt's office, for he had an office above the firehouse. I so remember that and all the back streets, back parts of Disneyland.

There were times when Walt would come in and watch us perform. He'd come in on a set very unobtrusive. We were all sort of in awe of him because we knew he was the boss. Walt was the artistic genius behind the studio. He still had a very large grasp of what we did as kids, yet what he said was law.

I can remember seeing him in the hall and we were always just very respectful of him. Of course, he knew us all by name—pretty easy for him to remember, as our names were on our sweaters.

As a Mouseketeer I would do the ins and outs for the newsreels. I would do introductions straight through, there was no cuts. Which is a lot of verbiage. Any mess ups, you have to start all over right from the start. One time, Walt Disney was standing right next to the camera, which made me nervous and I kept blowing my lines. Finally, I asked the AD if maybe Mr. Disney could possibly just move a little bit to the right so he would be out of my eye line, because he was making me nervous. One of the clever PR people for the show got wind of this and the next thing in the paper was Mouseketeer throws Walt Disney off set. Walt had a great sense of humor.

I'm grateful for Disneyland, because it gets to be part of my history. I love going down there at Christmastime with my wife and we just walk along the streets with the lights and it just brings back really such good memories. It's really fond to think back.

Tommy Cole

Lucille Martin
Walt Disney's Receptionist

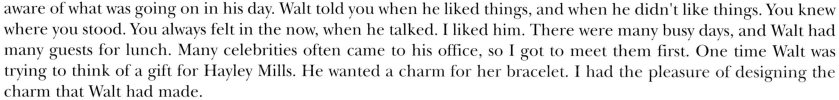

It was Friday afternoon and I needed a job. I drove up to the Disney Studios without an appointment and there was a guard at the gate, Johnny Polk. I said, "I'd like to find a job." He got on the phone and said, "I have an applicant here." They said to send me in. I went into personnel; they interviewed me. And hired me on that same day.

I walked in Monday morning and they sent me to the office of Donna LeVoy, in publicity. I worked there for a few weeks and also for Bonar Dyer, who was the head of labor relations. I was then sent to Walt's office.

The typical day started at 8 a.m. with Walt. Walt was very, very special. Walt would stay after work was over, and talk about his day. He made us very much aware of what was going on in his day. Walt told you when he liked things, and when he didn't like things. You knew where you stood. You always felt in the now, when he talked. I liked him. There were many busy days, and Walt had many guests for lunch. Many celebrities often came to his office, so I got to meet them first. One time Walt was trying to think of a gift for Hayley Mills. He wanted a charm for her bracelet. I had the pleasure of designing the charm that Walt had made.

Walt was very personable, and he wanted me to call him by his first name. I was used to saying "sir." Particularly with Walt, I kept saying, "sir." And he would say, "No, Walt." So one day he gave me a little drawing, showing a little girl marching, with a placard that said, "Down with sir."

I couldn't believe that I could have so much fun and enjoy my job so much and they paid me besides!

Walt's "Down with Sir" drawing

Courtesy of Lucille Martin

Interior of Yale and Towne Lock Shop

Local Sheriff and cast member compare firearms

Mell outfitted for a day of photography

Holiday of Many Nations Parade

**Fess Parker and C.V. Woods presents key to Disneyland
to then Vice President Richard Nixon and his family**

Hank Williams family enjoys a day at the park

Early morning in Disneyland

Two young guests enjoy the view of the Mark Twain Steamboat

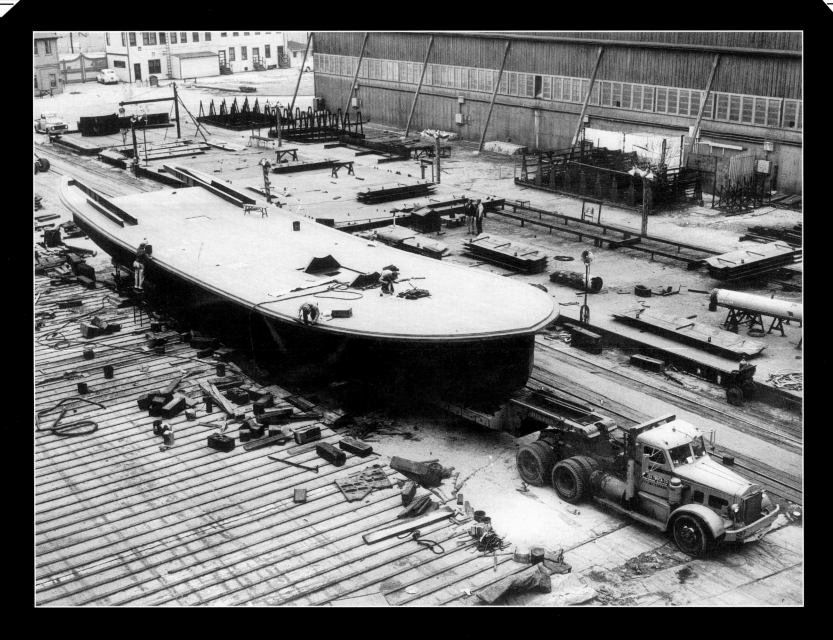

Mark Twain Steamboat hull being towed from Todd Shipyard

Mark Twain hull arrives at Disneyland

**Smokestacks
are placed
on the
Mark Twain**

Walt inspects the paddle wheel of the Mark Twain

Rivers of America encircle Tom Sawyer Island

**Fess Parker stands
guard outside
Davy Crockett Arcade**

Fess Parker

Actor: Starred in the following Disney films and TV projects:
Davy Crockett, King of the Wild Frontier series; Old Yeller; Westward Ho the Wagons

My journey to Disneyland began in August of 1954. I recorded the "Ballad of Davy Crockett" in August of 1954 right after the wonderful Walt Disney had placed me under a personal contract himself. I had my little guitar and I sang a song that I'd written about the railroads. It's called "Lonely." Well, I guess I convinced Walt that I was some sort of a singer, because he assigned me over to record the "Ballad of Davy Crockett" as a promotional record.

One thing about doing the movies—it was a frantic time. We made the first mini-series as far as I know. *King of the Wild Frontier, Davy Crockett Goes to Congress* and *Davy Crockett and the River Pirates.* Buddy Ebsen, Billy Bankwell, Basil Razdale, Kenneth Topey, Don McGallen, those were the principals.

Buddy Ebsen was a dancer, really, before I was born. It was a struggle for me, even though it was a fairly simple routine. Finally the big day came and we were put on our horses. We galloped into Frontierland and got down and did a folk dance and some chitter chatter. Later in the morning, the event that I'm proud of, is that Walt Disney asked me to ride alongside him on one of his horses in the very first parade down Main Street. I was extremely honored to do that and I think of it warmly.

On opening day there were so many people! It was like the sensation of being one of the sardines in their tin can. You walked around with your arms pinned down to your side. Of course, Buddy and I couldn't go anywhere.

I found Walt to be a very interesting and fun guy. He would come down to the set, I would be working, and we'd sit down in a couple chairs on the set and talk. Walt was a great man and we had some great times.

Fess Parker

"Lonely"
by Fess Parker

About sundown along a dusty street in a little western town
oil lamps are being lit,
folks are settin' down to supper and the laughter of children still at play
can be heard.
But at the far end of the street,
down at the depot house,
a still figure of a cowboy can be seen
listenin' to the fadin' sounds of a train far out on the prairie.

Oh lonely, lonely as I can be.
Lost my pal, I lost my gal. I'm lonely.
Gonna catch a train never comin' back
'cause I'm lonely.

Oh lonely, lonely as I can be.
My tale is of love, a pretty young maid and two young men
of a love for two and a loss of a friend that's my story
beginning and end.

Oh lonely, lonely as I can be.
I lost my pal. I lost my gal. I'm lonely.
Gonna catch a train never comin' back
'cause I'm lonely.

Yo lonely, lonely as I can be.
Lost my pal. I lost my gal. I'm lonely.
Gonna catch a train never comin' back
'cause I'm lonely. Yo, lonely.

**The Flora Dora girls and Can-Can dancers
perform at the Golden Horseshoe Revue**

Wally Boag

Comedian of the Golden Horseshoe Revue from 1955 - 1982
Consulted in development of Disneyland attractions, including
The Haunted Mansion and The Enchanted Tiki Room

It's hard to believe that it's been almost 50 years since we opened Disneyland. I was there and I remember all the things that happened on July 17th when Walt stood at the flagpole and dedicated the park. And we were off and running.

I had just joined the Disneyland family a few months before. Donald Novis, a fine Irish tenor I had worked with in a number of shows in Australia, called one day to tell me that Walt was going to build this place and needed a comic for a show in his soda pop saloon. I went over to the studio and did my nightclub act for him. I did some eccentric dancing, a little ventriloquism with my friend "George," played the bagpipes, and then finished with some balloon animals.

Walt's version of that day is that he told me this was going to be a family show. I told him I could clean the act up. I guess he believed me because he signed me to a two-week contract and I stayed for 27 years.

Those early days were great! Walt was always out front leading the parade and we knew we were part of something that was quite special—something that had never been done before. You'd see Walt all over the park and he loved to show you what he was thinking of next.

I ran into him one day over by the castle and he said, "Come on over here, I want to show you what I'm going to do in Tomorrowland." He pointed out where he was going to build a mountain, put in a submarine ride and expand the monorail. He had the enthusiasm and energy of a kid getting ready for Christmas.

We were lucky that he loved The Golden Horseshoe Review. Whenever he arrived at the park and parked his car behind City Hall, we'd get a call letting us know he was on the property and to reserve his box for him because he would stop by sometime during the day to see the show. And he was a great audience. He knew my act better than I did and he often had suggestions about how I could improve it. One day he said to me, "Why don't you package those balloons and sell them at the bar after each show." So, I did and I sold a ton of them.

continued on next page

One day I got the idea of doing a gunfight out in front of the Horseshoe. I set it up with the Frontierland lawman, Marshall Lucky Loredo, and we did it. I'd call him out into the street and force him to draw. Of course, I would lose and he would haul me off to "jail." Walt saw us do the gunfight one day and he loved it. "Do that anytime you can," he said. Eventually, he hired a couple of professional "cowboys" to do it.

After the park had been open for a few months, Walt signed a contract with ABC radio to produce a daily program called "Your Happy Holiday." We would find a family on its way into the park in the morning and ask them to be guests on the show. After they'd been in Disneyland for a couple of hours, we'd have them come over to the Horseshoe so I could ask them questions about what they'd seen (I was the emcee). It also gave us an opportunity to feature various celebrities who were in the park that day. We had plenty of them. President Eisenhower was in the audience one day and I called his grandson up on the stage and gave him the balloon animal. As he was going back to his seat, I handed him a bunch of balloons and said, "Here, give these to your grandfather and show him how to make an animal. It'll make him a big man in the neighborhood." I guess Ike liked the gag—he laughed.

One of the great things about working for Walt was that he let you wear a number of different hats. He often knew what you could do before you knew it. After I had been at the Horseshoe for a year or so, he asked me to spend some time doing some script and show development. That played out in a number of ways. I planned and did the entire stunt work for Fred McMurray when he was filming *The Absent Minded Professor*. At one time Walt was thinking of putting a Chinese restaurant on Main Street with a Confucius theme. We were working on some wonderful bits of business for the animated dragon we were going to have there. It didn't work out for a number of reasons, but it morphed into what is now the Tiki Room. Fulton Burley and I developed a script for those crazy birds and then we voiced them. I still find myself lapsing into my Jose' person—especially when I pass through my kitchen at home and talk to my parrot. He loves Jose. So, for me it was a great run at Disneyland.

Pleasant buffoonery to you all!

Wally Boag

Wally Boag (center) and cast of the Golden Horseshoe Revue

Sam McKim
IMAGINEER, DISNEY LEGEND

A Memorial Tribute to Sam McKim

By Carlene Thie

Sam McKim was a person no one can forget. Not just because of his contributions to Disneyland, but for his contributions to others. Sam was a gentleman, but also a gentle man—something that attracted everyone. A rare individual who gave freely, Sam often gave without expectation of receiving anything back. He was intelligent, friendly, humble, and charming all rolled into one.

Sam was born in Vancouver, British Columbia in 1924. His family moved to Los Angeles in 1935 which lead him to become a child actor. Sam worked with the best of them, John Wayne, Gene Autry, Spencer Tracy, James Cagney, Rita Hayworth, and even with his dear friend Jane Withers. He worked in many films, including, *Hit the Saddle, Painted Stallion* and three B-westerns with John Wayne.

Acting wasn't enough for Sam. He became a US citizen to serve in World War II and the Koran War and he received several medals for his service. After letting his acting career go, Sam moved on to what would be one of his more well known adventures, Disneyland.

Sam began working for Walt Disney's W.E.D. Enterprises (now Walt Disney Imagineering) in 1954, as an imagineer, doing the original sketches for Disneyland's Main Street, Frontierland, and Golden Horseshoe Revue. He also created a variety of sketches of Tom Sawyer Island, the concept drawing for the Haunted Mansion, Great Moments with Mr. Lincoln, as well as Disneyland's first large souvenir map. Early work for Disney television and films includes *The Gnome-Mobile, Johnny Tremaine, Zorro, The Shaggy Dog,* and *In Search of the Castaways*.

Sam's life took many different roads. Influencing many people with his loving spirit, Sam always put everyone and everything thing in front of himself. Sam touched my life in so many ways, he always seemed to have the greatest stories, the best memory, and the fondest things to say about everyone. I have never met a man who has done so much and given so much and yet stayed so humble and meek. If there is one thing I can do in remembrance of Sam, its to be as loving and forgiving as he was.

Brian McKim

Son of the late Sam McKim, legendary Disney Imagineer

"It all started with a Mouse!" is a famous quote from Walt Disney. Well, it all started at Disneyland, as far as millions of visitors at the world famous park are concerned! This is where baby boomers like me grew up with warm memories of Disneyland. I was fortunate enough to live somewhat near the park (within forty miles). I was also fortunate that I had two great parents (one who also happened to work for Walt) who took my brother and me to Disneyland every year, sometimes twice or three times a year!

I remember as a kid almost bursting with anticipation while waiting in line to enter the park. (Never mind that long trek down the Golden State Freeway! What made the drive more fun was who ever saw the Matterhorn first won a quarter from my dad.) Walking down Main Street was magical, even if as a kid you didn't know why. (Even a kid like me noticed there wasn't litter or chipped paint anywhere!)

I loved going onto Tom Sawyer Island, riding the pack mules at Rainbow Ridge, watching cartoons in the Mickey Mouse Club Theater during the summer, floating on the saucers in Tomorrowland; hanging above the crowds in the sky buckets and having the best banana spilt at the Carnation Plaza. Unfortunately, all these attractions or restaurants are gone now.

A couple of other memories stand out in my childhood. One was having a framed Disneyland Map hanging over my bed when I was young. I would pour over the map for hours, always ending up finding my dad's initials (S.M.) hidden in the foliage in the lower right corner of the map.

The other memory is almost meeting Walt one day. My mom dropped me off at W.E.D. Enterprises (now called Walt Disney Imagineering or W.D.I.). My dad and I had a few minutes before lunchtime so he suggested we go by Walt's office to introduce me to his boss. Unfortunately, Walt was off to another meeting and I was never to meet him.

Walt, along with his brother Roy, and many hand-picked artists built Disneyland with a vision to bring a "theme park" to those who have an imagination and a childlike enthusiasm for life.

Every time I visit Disneyland many great memories return and now I find myself carrying on similar traditions with my family. Thanks Walt, and thanks Dad for building the happiest place on earth!

All my Best

Brian McKim

**The Mark Twain takes us back to the adventures of Huckleberry Finn's days;
left to right: Tom Nabbe, Gray Chase, Hugh Allen**

Rivers of America from Indian Village

The Frito Kid dominates the view of Casa de Fritos

**Chris Winkler &
Perva Lou Smith
with Walt
at
Grand Opening of
Tom Sawyer Island**

Walt overlooks pouring
of water from the
Mississippi River
into
Rivers of America

Walt enjoys a day fishing at Catfish Cove

Bird's eye view of the park

Ollie Johnston
Disney Animator
Sleeping Beauty, Snow White and the Seven Dwarves, Bambi, Pinocchio, Lady and the Tramp, Alice in Wonderland, The Fox and the Hound, Fantasia, 101 Dalmatians, The Aristocats, The Jungle Book, Mary Poppins, The Rescuers

Photo courtesy of Ollie Johnston

It was wonderful to work with Walt Disney. He knew when the ideas were good, he helped make the ideas, and he used all his helpers who could create. And it so happened to be that I was one of the lucky ones.

It all began when I started my first class at Stanford, while I was sitting in the quad, this head comes around the post and says, "My name is Frank Thomas." I had never heard of him. He was there waiting to go to class, too. As it turned out, Frank Thomas and I became great friends. The first two years we were in school there, we palled around together and every time there was a class for drawing we would do it together.

We remained good friends and eventually after two years at Stanford Frank left to go to art school down south. It had been a while since I had seen him, so I went down with Stanford's football team to see what he was doing. After talking with Frank, I decided to talk with the dean at Stanford to see if I could graduate by going to an art school down there. He said, "Oh, sure, I can arrange that because you've been to all the other classes." About six months later I was drawing all these pretty girls and enjoying myself, having night classes, and everything was wonderful. When this guy came up to me and said, "Walt Disney wants you." I said, "I don't even know who he is."

So they took me to Walt Disney's place. That was an old, little outside school. I'm guessing I went there for two or three years. Then they just transferred to a big school in the main building at Disney where Walt Disney was. So I became part of that.

As I worked there I fell in love with making pictures where you understood and felt what the character was thinking. That seemed to make everybody very excited. Frank Thomas and I worked side-by-side there. Frank worked out his characters by being very intelligent. I worked mine out by feeling. I could feel how the people would feel and I would draw that. That's how I became what you'd call sort of famous.

When I worked on *Fantasia,* I did one thing I really loved. It was a section where the little cupids dress up the girls; all these girls that I had drawn came to life so they put hats on them and they did all kinds of things with them until they were all dressed up. People loved that. I also worked on *Cinderella, Alice in Wonderland* and *Sleeping Beauty.* Plus I worked on the *Jungle Book* picture. I did some Blue and Mogley. That was wonderful. I worked on the scene in *The Jungle Book* where the boy followed the girl up into the village and she keeps looking back. Walt said to me, "Boy, that's sexy, Ollie." So Walt loved that, and we left that in. The thing Walt had said was, "When you do that picture, whatever you do, don't read the book." I loved doing that picture. That was Walt's last picture.

Walt was always looking for the best ideas. And he had good ideas himself. He wasn't like anybody else. The first thing I ever did was a drawing of *Pinocchio.* And Walt heard about it. This was at the old studio. I was over there loafing, I'm sorry to say, talking to the two girls in the room next to Walt's when Walt comes out and says, "Boy, I sure like those Pinocchios you're doing." And he went back in his room.

Ollie Johnston 2004

Opening day was great. I loved that they had a steam train that ran around the whole place. It was a hot day, but wonderful for me. The newspaper people didn't like it at all. But by the end of three weeks, the newspaper guys had been back and were raving about the place, how wonderful it was. It was just that first day things wouldn't go right. I still remember the wonderful buildings; the whole place was like heaven.

I remember when Walt told me I was one of the nine old men someone trusted. That was very special. I love the man. He was so great to work with.

Columbia hull at Fowler's Harbor

Construction of the Columbia deck

Walt oversees the
Navy's tradition, as
Admiral A.C. Richmond
and his wife presents a
ship's Bible to the
Columbia's acting skipper

Gretchen Richmonds,
wife of
Admiral A.C. Richmond,
christens the Columbia
as Walt looks on

**Jimmy Durante performs
live radio from
Indian Village**

Grand Canyon diorama gets Navajo blessing

**Walt and Fred Gurley
approaching
ceremony stands**

Walt meeting "Chico" of the Santa Fe Railroad

Disneyland stage and pack mules round the bend in Frontierland

**Mule Riders head
out on an adventure to
Rainbow Ridge**

Art Linkletter
Veteran Television Personality

Walt Disney and I were friends. Even before Disneyland was conceived, Walt asked me to be his assistant in the presentation of programs at the Winter Olympics at Squaw Valley. I went up and lived with him and we became truly good friends. I emceed the programs for the officials and for the athletes. And with his power, he brought up the stars. We put on shows just for the inner Olympics, not for attendees.

Walt asked me to go with him to visit the Stanford Research people, who were going to pick the place where Disneyland would be built. As I drove down to Orange County, I thought, why are we going down there to put up some merry-go-rounds?

When Walt later asked me to emcee the opening ceremony and all, we worked out a deal. I was over at his house at a party when he said, "Art, I'd like to talk to you about emceeing the opening... shall I start with your agents? I can't afford to pay you really what you should get and I don't want to be bargaining with you and stuff. We're good friends." I replied, "Well, Walt, I don't have an agent, never had one and never will have one. You could do something for me. I'd like to have a concession for the sale of all film and cameras in Disneyland for 10 years. I'll pay your regular concession fee." So I got that. Which of course, was worth several million dollars.

Walt and I were friends even before we did the opening. Walt asked to be invited to all my dinner parties because they were some of the few that were small and he knew there wouldn't be photographers and press agents present. Our families were very similar. We were not typical Hollywood families. Walt and I would go down for a weekend at Palm Springs, and sit on the front porch and read the paper. No hoopla, no stuff.

The thing that is characteristic of my life is that I was always venturing to do something that I had never done before, which would open doors to a new life. It began in college when I was studying to be an English teacher and writing a column for the college paper. I was asked if I would write a musical comedy and I did. I've done the same thing all the way through my life. I take on jobs that are big and at risk and I've failed, got fired, lost jobs. But I was always willing to get higher and see what the next hill was. I have a little piece of poetry that I use in my talks. It goes like this:

> I never want to be what I want to be
> Because there's always something out there yet for me.
> I get a kick out of living in the here and now,
> But I never want to feel I know the best way how.
>
> Because there's always one hill higher with a better view,
> Something waiting to be learned I never knew.
> So 'til my days are over never fully fill my cup
> Let me go on growing, growing up.

That's my motto. And that's how I live. That's what I do.

Walt Disney, Art Linkletter and guests

Sam McKim
IMAGINEER, DISNEY LEGEND

Jungle Cruise ready to depart

Don Knotts

Actor: Starred in the following Disney films:
The Apple Dumpling Gang; Gus; No Deposit, No Return;
Herbie Goes to Monte Carlo

Strangely enough I didn't do a Disney movie until I was about 50. I started out as a ventriloquist as a kid, and then I went on to doing a radio show for five years for Bobby Benson. I was 25 years old and I played an old man in a western. Then there was the Steve Allen Show on Sunday night where I would do the nervous man routine. I just would shake and he'd say, "Are you nervous?"

And I'd go, "Nope." And it always made the audience laugh.

It was the Andy Griffith Show that was the most fun of anything in the business. I had a lot of fun working on it.

I'd been making a lot of pictures, but Disney didn't call me until they came up with a picture called *The Apple Dumpling Gang*. They wanted Tim Conway and I to do these inept outlaws together. This was my first Disney picture, and I went on to do five more for Disney. It was the *Apple Dumpling Gang* that started the thing for Tim and I. Before that, we had never worked together.

When I worked with Tim on the Disney pictures Tim would do something in the middle of a scene you didn't know he was going to do and it would just crack you up. I ruined a lot of takes by laughing, and that was the real fun. Tim is a character, no question about it. It was really fun to work at Disney. I enjoyed it a lot because it's just a fun place to work.

I've had a big, long, long career for sure. Still knocking around a little bit, not as much as I used to, of course. And I love still working with the Walt Disney Company even to this day.

Don Knotts

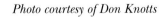

Tim Conway

Actor: Co-starred in the following Disney films:
The Apple Dumpling Gang, The Shaggy D.A.

Photo courtesy of Tim Conway

I have six children, so I lived at Disneyland. Not the day it opened, but early on when the children were big enough to go to Disneyland, I took everybody. My best recollection is when the ghost house first opened. I've always been one never to go to the front of the line. I always taught my kids that you stay in line and you buy a ticket. So we were in line for about an hour and a half to get into the new ghost house and my second youngest, Pat, just as we got to the entrance, decided to put his head through the two bars in the railing and got it stuck. So we had to call the engineers and they eventually pried him out. By that time he was all too scared to go in so we never have been in the ghost house, but I hear it's very, very frightening.

Working for Disney is a very unusual experience. It is the best place in the world. It truly is a magic land. You come onto the studio grounds and you have lunch with Mickey and the band's playing; it was a phenomenal place to work. I enjoyed some of the best times in the business at Disney. And I got to work with some of the best people. Don Knotts, is one.

We did *The Apple Dumpling Gang* together. It became one of the highest grossing pictures for Disney at the time, outside of *Mary Poppins*. I consider the quality of work as the best thing I ever did, and the most enjoyable thing I ever did as far as pictures are concerned. As an example, there's a scene early on in *The Apple Dumpling Gang* when we're trying to lasso Bill Bixby. I threw the lasso and it went straight up in the air and came down and draped over my hat and face. Don just looked at me. I said, "Well, maybe we'll get him some other time." And he just made a uh, hmmm. If I stood there from now until then or then until now, I could never throw that rope and have it land that way agian. And Don being the comic engineer that he is, never broke or never laughed or never did anything, he just went on with the scene like that was part of the show. Now, if it hadn't been Don, we'd have had to re-do that, but that's the scene that's in the movie.

The Disney crew built the firehouse set early for us to practice with because it was such a long scene. They paid us to come in a week early and to work out this ladder scene. Don and I would go there every day and we knew we were supposed to work out this ladder thing, but we would talk about the old days and Steve Allen and show business and everything. We never even thought about the ladder thing until one day they said, "Okay, we're going to be shooting this afternoon."

When they came down the director said, "Okay, what have you and Don worked out?"

I said, "Well, Don actually has worked out most of it, so he'll tell you what it is."

But Don had no idea. So we started working it out as we were talking. I said to Don, "Didn't you say do this?" So we did. "And I think I told you, Don, to go this way..." We actually worked it out while we were talking to the director. And it obviously turned out to be one of the better scenes in the picture. It was nothing more than happy times working there.

I've worked with the biggest stars in this business, been friends with some, and kept that friendship through the years. I wouldn't change a thing that I have done. The successes, the failures, the low parts, the high parts, I wouldn't change anything at all.

Disney is like going to Mayberry. Don't you wish you could live in an atmosphere where everything was wonderful and you didn't have to lock your door at night and people were marvelous in town and the biggest event of the year was the pickle contest. It's a marvelous fantasy world that was created by Walt and it has remained that. The whole place is just phenomenal.

Tim Conway

Sam McKim

IMAGINEER, DISNEY LEGEND

Yale Gracey

By Beverly Gracey, widow of Yale Gracey
Disney Imagineer from 1939- 1975

My late husband Yale was the only child of a family in the diplomatic service and so he was raised all over the world. He was born in China. He lived in Spain and Portugal, went back to China and then to Japan.

Yale moved to California, where he went to Art Center for four years. After graduating from Art Center he wasn't sure what he was going to do. He got a portfolio together and just did some things. Went to a polo match in Will Rogers's Polo Field. Walt played polo quite a bit at that time and a friend of Yale's introduced him to Walt.

Walt talked to Yale about being an artist and said, "Well, we always can use new talent. Get your stuff together and I'll interview you."

Disney hired Yale in 1939, and put him to work in the layout department for the animated classics. He also helped design the background of animated short films, like an art director that designs the colors, the backgrounds and figures out where the characters are going to move and so forth.

Walt came up with the idea of doing something different. He didn't share it with anyone; he just picked out seven couples and flew them in the private plane to Montreal and said to take notes and observe what the attractions are and particularly notice the restaurants and the layout. Everyone had to turn in a little report for our wonderful week there. And nothing ever was said about it or anything.

Nobody knew that there was a Disneyland planned. Then a friend of ours who lived in Orange County asked Yale how come Disney was buying up property. Yale didn't know anything about it and asked around and nobody else seemed to know anything about it.

Over a period of probably a year Walt was buying up orange fields. Not with his name on it at all. It was done through different companies, different names, and different people. All of a sudden, they had the package for Disneyland. They took out the orange fields and so forth. It was quite a shock to everybody because we didn't know anything about it. Walt kept it very, very quiet because the price would go up and he didn't want anyone to know about it.

continued on page 106

Yale Gracey makes final touches in Haunted Mansion
Photo courtesy of Beverly Gracey

Yale headed a small section of the imagineer department beginning with two people, working eventually to five or six. He designed and came up with all the special effects; created illusions, such as the "999 grim grinning ghost," the lighting, and anything that was like a candle that looks like it's burning. At Disneyland he worked mostly on the Haunted Mansion and the Pirates of the Caribbean ride.

Yale was called on to do a lot of things at Disneyland. He never revealed them, and how these things were done were never written up because they didn't want anybody to steal the methods. Walt would come through, sometimes with Roy, but mostly himself and secretaries to take notes, and he'd say, "Well, guys, I like it, it's good. I think you're on the right track, but I think you can do better." And so they would go back to the drawing board and back to lighting and noise and sound and effects.

When they created the pirate ride they had to have a clearance from the fire department. They had purchased the fire as a special effect, and it's done with lighting and sound and all of that. They brought fragrances for the gardenia and all of that. So they bought a smoke fragrance and as you went through the flames in the boat the smoke fragrance was very prevalent. The fire department would not pass the effect because it was too real and they said that you'd have heart attacks and people screaming to get out of the boat. So they made them take the fragrance out and just leave the crackling fire. When they opened the pirate ride, it was a big success because of the fire and everything.

With Disneyland no expense was spared because it would last and it would glitter more, and so the best was used. All the best things were always used. There was real gold leaf on the big ship, for you couldn't get that same effect with gold paint.

Walt loved putting on old clothes, going down and just being one of the mob to hear what they said. One time Yale bumped into Walt dressed as one of the attendants of the jungle river ride, helping people off the boat. Walt just loved hearing what people were saying and watching their expressions.

Beverly Gracey

Yale Gracey starts the pace off between the "Dueling Ghosts"
Photo courtesy of Beverly Gracey

Teller
Magician from the duo Penn & Teller

When I was a small kid I saw all about the opening of Disneyland on TV. I desperately wanted to go. That year my father had a good winter in his commercial-art lettering business, and took my mother and me on a three-week cross-country trip from Philadelphia to Los Angeles. We did the Sequoias, the Grand Canyon, and finally, we arrived in Los Angeles.

As we headed for Disneyland, I dozed off. When I woke up, my parents reported to me that they'd gotten to the gates of Disneyland and it wasn't open to the pubic yet. I was so foggy from sleep, I forgot to be really disappointed. The next time I went, I was grown up.

As you might imagine, I'm a long-standing fan of the Haunted Mansion, mainly because it contains such beautiful use of the classic Peppers Ghost in the ballroom scene. In fact, this version is even more classic than that. It harks back to Dircks, who actually invented the principle in 1858. The very idea that the lame amusement park Spook House with its air-jets to blow up the girls' skirts, could become such a work of art just thrills me.

Teller

A view of the "Native Village" on Jungle Cruise ride

Aerial view of Adventureland with Main Street above

Approaching Schweitzer Falls on the Jungle Cruise

David Pacheco
A Disney Creative Director, 1980 to present

Photo courtesy of David Pacheco

When I was a child my father would take me to Disneyland and to see Walt's animated films as often as we could. He enjoyed the films himself and my sister and I were a great excuse for him to tag along. So I grew up with Disney. From a very early age, I knew I wanted to work for Walt Disney. I didn't really understand who he was but I did know that he brought an incredible sense of imagination and magic into people's lives. Certainly, into mine. Sounds cliché, I know, but it's difficult to describe what Walt and his artists brought to the world through film and Disneyland.

Looking back, I see how absorbed I was in all the details of the characters and stories. After seeing one of Walt's films or time spent at Disneyland, out would come the pad of paper and color pens and I would try to render (as close as I could recall) scenes from the film or the interior of the attractions. On visits to the park, my parents sometimes bought me a souvenir character figurine. Most times they didn't look "correct" to me so I would bring out the model paints and repaint them. The same went for the Disney books. My parents would get so angry. I didn't understand, "artistic interpretation," then. I just wanted to make the illustrations look, "better," as I remembered them. I imagined working for Walt on his cartoons.

I still have several school books with characters that animate on the corners when you flip the pages (math was never my forte). I also wanted to create a line of figurines that would look better than the ones I had. And books too. That would save a lot of time repainting! My first professional animation was at the Hanna Barbera Studios. I worked there for two years and still dreamed of working for the Disney Studios but didn't have much confidence in my abilities. One day, I had a run-in with my director and walked out. I drove over to the Disney lot and pulled up at the front gate. I didn't have an appointment with anyone so the guard didn't let me in. I told him I just wanted to leave my portfolio. He told me to leave it and he'd forward it to the animation department for me. I thought, "Well. That's that. Now what?" The next day they called me and asked when I could start.

I began work in feature animation in September of 1980 as a "breakdown artist" and in a year became an "assistant animator." Two years later I was promoted to full animator. I worked on many wonderful projects in my nine

continued on page 114

Drawing by David Pacheco

years in animation. For example, *Who framed Roger Rabbit?* and *The Little Mermaid*. My favorite project was reconstructing the lost sequences from *Snow White and the Seven Dwarfs*. I was given carte blanche to search where I wanted for anything related to this classic film. Some of the animation drawings were found at the bottom of the dumbwaiter shaft in the basement of the Ink and Paint building. They most likely had been there for years and were covered with dust and grease. No one knew they were there. There were folders and folders of drawings that had fallen off the sides of the platform. There were literally hundreds of rough animation drawings of the dwarfs but unmarked as to what scene or sequence they were from. I put them together by characters and brought out a copy of the final script. I would take a scene of Bashful, for example, and then take all the Bashful dialog and literally "read" the character's lips to the words to bring all this together. A few weeks before this sequence was to air on television as part of the 50th anniversary of the film the original dialog recordings were uncovered in a closet in the Music building. For the first time in 50 years, the dwarves spoke again. That was a real thrill!

While working with Disney Publishing, my supervisor called me in and told me that a new, "collectibles" department was opening up and they were looking for someone who was familiar with all the characters. I was to go downstairs and help out, but I was told, "Not until 5:00 when your day is done and don't spend more than three hours with them." Well, those three hours have turned into about 14 years now working with Walt Disney Art Classics.

In my career with Disney I've worked on all of the things I imagined that I would in my childhood. I worked on "making cartoons" and on illustrations for hundreds of books from comics to high-end coffee table books. I've helped to create several lines of Disney character sculptures and figurines and was given the honor of designing the 12 Disney character U.S. postage stamps, the characters being as I remember them to be. I hope. I have so much fun!

All the best,

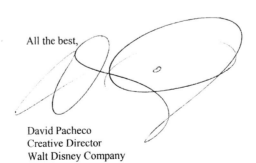

David Pacheco
Creative Director
Walt Disney Company

A view from Mell's perch in the sky

Skull Rock in Pirate's Cove

Walt's vision of the Sleeping Beauty Castle starting to form

Sleeping Beauty Castle moat not even part of the scenery yet

Willie Ito
Disney Animator
Lady and the Tramp

In June of 1954 I first stepped foot on the campus of the Walt Disney studios in Burbank. I had just graduated from City College of San Francisco. Using my student portfolio as a "ticket," I called and got an appointment with personnel.

It was a warm afternoon in Burbank. I was dressed in my San Francisco finest, wool slacks, tweed jacket, and even my necktie was a wool knit. My portfolio weighed a ton as I walked onto the studio lot. As I proceeded up Mickey Avenue towards the animation building, I could feel the perspiration streaming down my face. I entered the hallways of Disney, went to the elevator, and pressed the button for the fourth floor. As the door closed, it suddenly opened and standing before me was Walt himself. He was with another gentleman, in deep conversation, but as they stepped in Walt looked up and acknowledged my presence with a polite nod.

My meeting went well and I received the "Don't call us, we'll call you" response. Two weeks later, as I returned from my classes late one evening, I noticed that stuck in the door of my rooming house was a Western Union Telegram. I opened the letter expecting bad news. However, it was from the Walt Disney Productions personnel department asking me to report the following Monday for work.

That Monday I got to the studio early. I reported to a Johnny Bond and he sat me down and gave me an "in-between" test. After lunch, I was assigned to the "Lady" group. I thought that meant I was going into the ink and paint department, since the ladies dominated it. I quickly learned that *Lady and the Tramp* was in production and I was assigned to work on the "Lady" character.

During the production of *Lady and the Tramp* I got to know many future W.E.D. talent like Frank Armitage, Ken O'Brien, Marc Davis, as well as Rolly Crump (who is one true "fun guy"). The studio was a beehive of activity when a new project was in the works. Walt was in the planning stages of an amusement park—a play land of sorts. The phrase "theme park" was not yet coined. I wandered onto the back lot and, in one of the workshops, I saw large molds of the Dumbo ride, miniature trains, stagecoaches, huge blueprints on the walls, etc. It was teaming with activity. I got Walt's infamous eyebrow, since I was spotted more than a few times nosing around.

As more news of the progress of Disneyland trickled down to us in animation, there was curiosity, wonderment, and "Disney's folly" comments. More of us ventured upstairs where the W.E.D. group was working. John Hench and company had these wonderful paintings and sketches pinned on large storyboards lining the third floor hallways. We were now beginning to understand what it was all about. It was absolutely mind blowing what was being built.

Willie Ito

Drawing by Willie Ito

Floyd Norman
Disney Animator

I was headed south on the 5 freeway (then called Highway 101), for a class assignment when I spotted a construction site yards away for me. Huge earthmovers lumbered back and forth creating huge berms, and uprooting rows of orange trees. The students in my group had no knowledge of the construction project, and chose to ignore it. Yet, I was more than aware that this site was to be like none other the world had ever seen. This was the location of the most ambitious project Walt Disney had ever undertaken: the project called Disneyland.

I was not part of the celebrity and employee guess list that opening Sunday. Like most Americans, I watched the proceedings on black and white television from my living room. The host of the show was none other than Walt Disney himself who, along with his co-hosts, Ronald Reagan, Art Linkletter, and Robert Cummings, introduced us to the Magic Kingdom. The live telecast on ABC was not without several glitches, but it didn't matter. We were all too entranced with this magical theme park to notice any televised imperfections. Like so many Disney fans, I couldn't wait to visit Disneyland, so the very next day, I was on my way.

It's difficult to explain what it was like seeing Disneyland for the first time. Logically, I knew the park had been under construction for some time, but now all that logic seemed to disappear, and it was as if the park had suddenly appeared out of nowhere. Disneyland appeared before us as though it had materialized out of nothing but pixie dust. As our little group entered the park that opening week, it was truly an eye-popping experience! Everything was fresh and new, and it all seemed to have a magic sparkle. Saying the park was clean was an understatement. One could have eaten off the sidewalk—literally. In time, Disneyland would enjoy huge crowds, but this day attendance was good, yet not at all crowded. This gave the guest unobstructed views of the park, and it also meant there would be no long lines for rides. In many ways, it was the ideal time to visit Disneyland.

So much time has passed since my first visit 50 years ago, but I can see Disneyland as though it were only yesterday. The memories of that first visit remain fresh and clear to this day.

Construction view of Sleeping Beauty Castle and moat

A visit to Disneyland

continued from page 41

A VISIT TO DISNEYLAND

Public Relations Dept.
Disneyland, Inc.
1313 Harbor Blvd.
Anaheim, Calif.

Young and old will drive Tomorrowland's freeway of the future in the Disneyland Autopia. These miniature cars are gas driven. All drivers-- whether seven or seventy--must pass an Autopia Drivers' test before taking the automobiles out. Driving speed is kept down to eleven miles per hour with the use of mechanical governors, and all cars travel in the same dir- ection, so that the youngest driver is safe as he learns driving technique. Scaled-down speed boats in an island dotted waterway also offer thrilling rides in Tomorrowland.

A preview of future food service technique and atmosphere is offered in the modernistic restaurant.

The next land is Fantasyland. To the right of Tomorrowland and at the far end of Main Street, rising above the medieval battlements of moat and drawbridge, Sleeping Beauty's castle guards the entrance to the elusive land of fantasy.

Once over the bridge and winding through the castle, Sleeping Beauty is seen in the splendor of medieval array. A dungeon with rack and wheel and torture chambers, the large dining hall of the knights and other castle appointments are among the wonders passed before entering the courtyard.

Here King Arthur's carrousel beckons as the banners of returning knights wave victoriously in the breeze. Around the courtyard are buildings housing, among other things, the Peter Pan ride. In this "dark ride" guests board a pirate galleon to spend three exciting minutes soaring high over London, Never Never Land, Skull rock, and Captain Hook's hideway. Other characters of fantasy and fable are met in the Snow White ride, Mr. Toad's

-more-

A VISIT TO DISNEYLAND

Public Relations Dept.
Disneyland, Inc.
1313 Harbor Blvd.
Anaheim, Calif.

wild ride, the Mad Tea Party, Casey Jr. train and the Dumbo ride.

Light food and refreshments are offered from stands designed with the flair and color of a circus in Fantasyland. Here, too, is the unusual Pirate Ship restaurant, serving complete family meals.

Having toured Fantasyland and returned to the Plaza, a Frontierland visit is next in order. This land, beginning at Plymouth Rock and following Americans on their westward march, is entered through a log stockade. At its gate Indians of many tribes are weaving blankets and baskets, making pottery and selling souvenirs. Horses are shod at the blacksmith shop. The general store carries merchandise of the cheese, crackers and pickle-barrel period. Miners bring their "poke" into the assay office. Frontiersmen stop in at the "Golden Horseshoe," longest little bar in the world, for light refreshments and a frontier-days floor show. Here young cowpokes must resign themselves to parting with gunbelts, as all arms must be checked at the entrance in true frontier style.

Stage coaches carry passengers from Frontierland through the Painted Desert, pass an Indian encampment, ford a stream and go through a pine forest. Different coaches and wagons take different routes, which last from four to ten minutes.

It is at Frontierland that the "Mark Twain" docks, bringing with it the romance of early riverboats. The "Mark Twain" is a 105-foot stern wheeler typical of the boats that plied the Mississippi in 1900. It is built to 5/8 scale and accommodates 300 passengers on each trip down the "rivers of America."

A visit
to Disneyland

Aerial view of Sleeping Beauty Castle under construction

**Sleeping Beauty Castle with Chicken of the
Sea Pirate Ship Restaurant starting to take shape**

Ron Dias
Disney Animator and Art Director
Sleeping Beauty, The Little Mermaid

I'd like to start from the beginning, because I've been working with Disney for a long time and the beginnings were the really fun times because that's when Walt was still with us.

When I was a youngster I was always fascinated with animated film. I couldn't believe they could actually make things move, and that is what I wanted to do.

In my teens I would write to the studio asking questions, like what kind of art training should I take, with every single letter I ever wrote being answered. That's when I learned I should take as many anatomy classes as I could to help in understanding the figure, and knowing how it moves.

In high school, my art teacher told us of a national contest to design a children's stamp. She said, "It's a children's friendship stamp, and I'm going to make it a class project." So each of us designed one, and my stamp slogan was "Friendship is the Key to World Peace."

I was putting my third Disney portfolio together when one night I heard a knock at the door. The Valley Times, LA Times, and the Valley News, and others, were out front. There were cameras flashing, people asking me questions. "How does it feel to win?"

"Win what?" I said.

"The contest..." they replied.

"What contest?" Remembering I had gotten little bits of paper saying you're in the last 200 finalists, you're in the 150, you're in the... which I had not payed attention to.

They said, "The Children's Friendship Stamp."

"Oh, I won the stamp contest? Well, I'm tickled pink," is what I said.

Well, not realizing that when I was interviewed, I had mentioned to every single paper was that I wanted to work at Disney.

So, this all came out in the paper the next day. I got a call from the Disney Studios, telling me that they had read in the paper that I seriously wanted to work for them. And that's how it all started. Just a few days later, I was working at the studio. Because of the news, Walt knew who I was and would always say good morning to me, and if he had a hat, I think he tipped it.

It was such a wonderful time to work at Disney, with Marc Davis and the whole crew on *Sleeping Beauty*. I realized how much I could move people by doing what I did with the beauty, the magic, and the fantasy of animated film. The thing that makes *Sleeping Beauty* unique is that it's like a moving tapestry. It's like a medieval painting. And it's like no other film and no other film like it has ever been done since. It's graphically very design-y, decorative, and yet very renaisance-y looking film.

Walt never missed a beat about anything, and knew everything that was going on. Walt was very involved in animatronics at the park; the Lincoln project, Pirates Of the Caribbean, and the Haunted House at Disneyland. It was phenomenal.

I think the whole amazing thing about Disneyland was not only the growth happening and the innovative stuff, but also how clean this park was. It was spotless! We couldn't believe how something so humongous could be kept so clean at all times. We all appreciated that.

Ron Dias

RonDias

Ilene Woods
Voice artist for Cinderella,
from the Walt Disney animated classic, Cinderella

Courtesy of Ilene Woods

My introduction to Walt Disney and how I got the part of Cinderella was quite unusual. I was born to a dancing teacher in Portsmouth, New Hampshire. So, needless to say, I was around show business dancing and singing and on stage from the age of two. I loved it.

At the age of 14, my mother took me to New York for vacation and while we were there, we met the head of the local Portsmouth radio station. He wanted me to do an audition at ABC. I went into a little studio where I sang a couple of songs. I couldn't wait to get back out to see New York, which was my first visit to that city. While we were waiting at the elevator, I was told that the Eastern Program Director wanted to see me. He liked what he heard and offered me a job when I finished that year of school. He guaranteed me three nights a week on ABC if I would come back in the summer. So I started singing on ABC in New York at the age of 15.

I went from there to Don McNeil's Breakfast Club in Chicago. I was working with Eve Arden and Jack Carson when auditions for Cinderella came up. I received a call from two song writers I knew from New York, wanting to know if I would go into a studio and make a recording of a couple of songs they were presenting to the maker of a movie. The day after recording them I went back to work, where I received a call from my manager that Walt Disney wanted to meet me. I didn't know why. We met at the studio where we talked for a few minutes.

Walt said, "How would you like to be Cinderella?"
And I said, "Cinderella? I don't understand, Mr. Disney. I don't know what you're talking about."
He said, "I'm making a movie called Cinderella, the storybook character. Would you like to be Cinderella?"
And I said, "I would love to be."
Walt said, "Well, you are."

Walt had listened to the recording and not only had he bought the songs, but he wanted to know who was singing the songs on the recording. I worked on the movie for two and a half years.

One day when we were recording Walt said to me, "Ilene can you sing harmony with yourself?"

I said, "I don't think so Mr. Disney. I couldn't even whistle and hum at the same time."

Walt said, "I think we can do it."

Walt turned around to the engineer and said, "We can do it. I'm sure we can."

The engineer looked at him and said, "Well, if you say so, Walt. You have to tell me how, though."

Then Walt told him about layering voices. "Ilene will sing the first part, and then we'll layer and she'll sing the second part harmony."

We did it. By the time we were finished we had about six or seven-part harmony going. It was the first time it had ever been done. Patty Page hadn't yet made the recording where she sang harmony with herself that made her so famous. Walt Disney was the first to come up with a person harmonizing with themself.

That song turned out to be Cinderella scrubbing the floor.

Walt said, "I can see a soap bubble coming up and she sees her face in the soap bubble and that's another voice. Then I see another soap bubble coming up and she sees another face in the soap bubble reflection and that's another voice."

They did it until there were a million soap bubbles and when we came in a week later and heard the playback, it was just amazing. I had never heard anything like it in my life.

He was always coming up with wonderful ideas for the movie. He was such a nice man; truly one of the nicest and most brilliant people I ever knew. And like I said, the only true visionary I think I've ever known. I could have sat and listened to him all day long. He was just wonderful.

I saw such humility in Walt. He was only interested in the product and being satisfied with it himself and being happy with what was being done. He wasn't looking for people to fall to their knees and say, "Oh, Walt, you're wonderful, that was wonderful, oh, you should make millions with that." No, he was just happy to make it happen. He got joy from that, his ideas coming to life.

I was so thrilled with the movie itself. Having been a part of it and working with a man like Walt Disney was such a treat. I was 17 when I got the part. Not by auditioning, but by doing a favor for two friends. So I never hesitate to do favors for friends anymore.

Ilene Woods
"Cinderella"

Dean Jones

Actor

Courtesy of Dean Jones

The photograph at right was taken at Disneyland the day Mickey gave me one of the original "Herbies" from the film, *The Love Bug*. Although I've made 46 movies, the 10 films for Walt Disney stand out in my memory. *The Love Bug* was the top grossing film of 1969, a year that saw the release of *Midnight Cowboy, Butch Cassidy* and *The Sundance Kid,* and *Funny Girl*. Needles to say, "Herbie" and I have remained friends.

The first I heard about making *The Love Bug* was from Walt Disney himself. Walt visited the set of *Blackbeard's Ghost* and asked about a script I had sent him—the story of the first sports car ever imported into the United States.

"Do you have an option on the script?" Walt asked,

"No," I replied, "I just like the idea and think it would make a good Disney film.

Walt smiled. "I just bought a book called Car-Boy-Girl and I think you'll like it even better."

Two years later, Walt was no longer with us, but we made his "Car" movie, retitled it *The Love Bug,* and it leaped onto the list of all-time top ten grossing films, right next to *Gone With the Wind*!

Several times over the years, I've driven "Herbie" in Disneyland's Christmas Parade, and I'm always flooded with memories. It's hard to explain the success of that little movie, but Walt knew how to pick 'em—cars, actors and stories. And millions of people still miss his creative touch. So do I.

Photo courtesy of Dean Jones

Sleeping Beauty Castle cones being craned into place

Sam McKim
IMAGINEER, DISNEY LEGEND

**Sleeping Beauty Castle
painters group shot**

**Backside of Fantasyland with Chicken of the Sea Pirate Ship
and Casey Jr. Railroad**

Lady of the Lake leaves the dock

Close up view of Story Book Land

Matt McKim
Son of the late Sam McKim, legendary Disney Imagineer

I must have been around seven years old when my mom took me to the little park down the street from W.E.D. (now known as Walt Disney Imagineering or W.D.I.) to meet my dad for lunch. After eating I ran over to the swings to see how high I could go. After awhile of flying through the air at mach 1, I noticed my parents talking with a black haired lady. My dad called out to me to come over and meet her.

"Matt, I would like you to meet my friend Leota Toombs. She works in the model shop at W.E.D." my dad said.

I said it was nice to meet her, while shaking her hand.

My dad then added, "She's also the head in the crystal ball and the little talking woman that says 'hurry baaaack' in the Haunted Mansion."

I must have given her a scrutinizing squint, checking her out. When I caught my composure I replied, "Wow, it's really nice to meet you!"

After she left, I turned to my dad and said, "Okay Dad, who really was that lady?"

"Just as I said, Leota Toombs, the lady in the crystal ball," he replied.

I quipped back, "You can't fool me! Everybody knows that the lady in the crystal ball has white hair!

It took my parents a few minutes to explain that it was her face projected with fake white hair in the ball. Seven-year-olds can be so literal! I saw sweet Leota many times after that, and she became one of my top five favorite people at W.E.D.

All the best,

Matt McKim

Castle Neuschwanstien in Germany (inspiration for Sleeping Beauty Castle)
Drawing by Sam McKim

Alice in Wonderland from Matterhorn construction

Midget Autopia with Monorail construction

Lisa Davis

Voice artist for Anita in the Walt Disney animated classic The 101 Dalmatians

I first met Walt Disney when he was planning *Alice in Wonderland*. At that time instead of animating Alice, he had decided that he would have a live character that would play Alice and he would animate all of the characters around her. Walt brought me over from England and we did a lot of wardrobe tests and pre-work for *Alice in Wonderland*. He eventually realized it would be more expensive than the usual projects and he scrapped the whole idea.

Later when Walt Disney was planning *101 Dalmatians* he called on me again. In those days Zsa Zsa Gabor had a reputation for wearing furs and diamonds and was such an eccentric, he pictured Cruella as a Zsa Zsa Gabor-type of person. Because I had achieved a reputation to imitate her fairly well, he called me into the studio to read Cruella De Vil.

Walt had remembered me from when I was 12 years old, but now I was about 18 or 19. He brought me to one of the buildings and into a little room and seated me across from him with the script. I couldn't believe it was Walt Disney that I was sitting with because he had always had this aura of being a miracle worker.

So here I am sitting across from Walt Disney in the room and he is reading the role of Anita and I am reading the role of Cruella. Well, I first got into this a little bit and I heard the personality of Anita as opposed to what I was struggling to do to become Cruella. I realized that I was so much more Anita than I was ever a Cruella. How does one tell Walt Disney that he's made the wrong selection? I thought, I've got to tell him that he called me in for the wrong part. So I said, "Excuse me, Mr. Disney, I'm thrilled to be here. But as you read this part with me, I really feel that I'm much more Anita than I am Cruella."

Walt said, "Would you like to read Anita?"
"Oh, I'd love to. Could I?" I replied.
He said, "Yes. I'll play Cruella, you try Anita."
So we switched, and that's how I became Anita in *101 Dalmatians*.

It was and is to this day, probably the finest and the most wonderful job that I have ever done. It lives with me. I am still reaping incredible rewards.

Walt was very, very much in love with what he did and he loved the people who did it for him. Walt was very, very kind to the people who worked for him. His first line team of animators, they were all great friends. The young women who became the voices—Cathy Beaumont for Wendy, Alice and Mary Compton, Sleeping Beauty, myself—he took us on just like a daughter. Walt was very kind to us. It was a wonderful place.

Working with Walt Disney was a wonderful, wonderful experience. Disneyland was already built when he was filming *101*, but it wasn't complete, as it is never to be complete. He had one whole room with model layouts of all the new rides that he was planning. I remember him taking me into the room and showing with great joy those tiny versions of the rides. He had miniatures of every ride that he was planning for Disneyland.

I have wonderful memories of Mr. Disney and his kindness to me. I still love going to the Disney Studio and walking into the commissary, where I look over to where Walt's seat was. I have tender and loving memories of Walt Disney and the Studios.

Lisa Davis

**Sleeping Beauty Castle
with "Fantasy in the Sky"**

Sky Buckets and Viewliner train in Tomorrowland

TWA personnel posing for the camera

Sam McKim

IMAGINEER, DISNEY LEGEND

Moonliner being
craned into place

**Donna Reed
and family posing
for the camera**

Hello from the Autopia

Drivers enjoying Richfield's Autopia

1950

Walt and Charlie Pearson greet incoming helicoptor guests

FITTING CHAMBER

20,000 Leagues diving suits

Richard Fleischer
Director

Photo courtesy of Richard Fleischer

When Walt Disney asked me to direct Disney's first live-action film, *20,000 Leagues Under the Sea*, it caught me completely off guard. I couldn't understand why he would select me to direct, considering my father, Max Fleischer, was one of his biggest competitors in the animation world. Out of respect, I told Walt that I would have to ask my father for permission to take the job. I called my father in New York that evening to tell him about the offer. When I told him that Walt had asked me to direct *20,000 Leagues Under the Sea*, he said, "Of course you must take the job without any question!" He then said, "Give Walt a message for me. Tell him he has great taste in directors."

When it came time to direct the film, the first big problem we ran into was an unruly giant squid. It looked terribly phony and was falling apart in several places. The way it had been constructed was very poor. So Walt and I decided to go a completely different direction and revamp the creature. The first squid was officially fired. We then decided to shoot the sequence at night during a big storm at sea, instead of during the day in calm water. That way it gave a more realistic look to the whole thing. The result was very exciting.

Richard Fleischer

Nautilus model and matte paintings from 20,000 Leagues Under the Sea

Walt and Fred Gurley take Engine No. 3 on the inaugural run

Submarine Voyage track being fitted

Submarine Lagoon scenic elements

Tomorrowland Autopia surrounded by construction

Tomorrowland from the air

Inspection of the Submarine Voyage

Matterhorn looms behind Submarine Voyage

**Sky view
of the
Avenue of Flags**

Looking down on the Monsanto House of the Future

Monsanto Hall of Chemistry

Bell System showcased the America The Beautiful Theater

A view of Tomorrowland at Harbor Boulevard

A 1961 view of Disneyland from the air

Tim Conway

Don Knotts

Tommy Cole

Ron Dominguez

Wally Boag

Floyd Norman

Teller

Keith Murdoch

Dean Jones

Ron Dias

Lucille Martin

172

Matt McKim

Willie Ito

Ollie Johnston

Brian McKim

Ilene Woods

Fess Parker

Sam McKim

Ape
"The Actress"

Carlene Thie

Jack Lindquist

Dave Pacheco

Richard Fleischer

As people touched my life with their love of Disneyland, I realized I could contribute to their memories by creating these photo books which capture Disneyland's early history for everyone to enjoy. More importantly, by sharing these images, I am able to honor my grandfather, and his legacy as a photojournalist. Through these projects, I have met many wonderful people, and learned a great deal about Walt Disney and his dreams— for this I am very grateful.

Carlene Thie

Author and Publisher
Carlene Thie
with "Ape" April (Actress)

Vol. # 1

**A photographer's life with
Disneyland Under Construction**

Vol. # 2

**Disneyland's Early Years
Through the Eye of a Photographer**

Vol. # 3

**Disneyland
Seen Through a Photographer's Lens**

Vol. # 4

**Disneyland...
the Beginning**

I want to thank God and all those who have helped me in the process of
creating these volumes, especially my family.

Copyright 2005 - Ape Pen Publishing

*P.O. Box 691, Riverside, California 92502
ApePenPublishing.com*

*Printed in U.S.A.
by Jostens, Inc.
Marceline, Missouri*